No portion of this book may be reproduced in any form without written permission from the publisher or author, except as permitted by U.S. copyright law.

Text & Illustrations
Copyright © 2025
Kim Ray Malyszek

All rights reserved.

ISBN 979-8-9929303-9-9

First published 2025
SnowFish Publishing

www.abcsofmountainbiking.com

The ABCs of Mountain Biking

Written + Illustrated
by
Kim Ray Malyszek

A
Air Pump

air pumps put air into our bike tires

B Brakes

brakes slow down and stop our bikes

F

FRAME

frames are the main structure of our bikes

RIDE FUN RIDE FAST RIDE SAFE

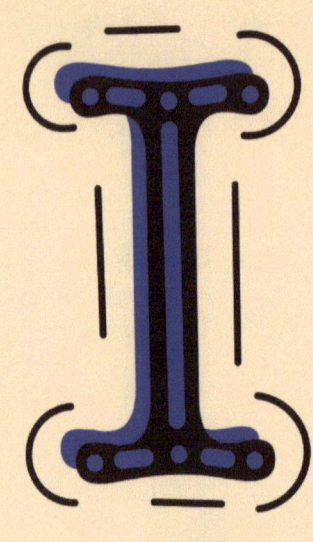

inspect your bike before riding to make sure nothing is loose and to check that there is enough air in your tires

Inspect

L
light

lights help us see when its dark

Wheels

wheels roll and move our bikes forward